FATHER OF THE MOVEMENT

Father of the Movement

Unheard of Learning

Contents

Acknowledgments

To my student Editors, Ramon and Deajane: no one else could have added to this work the way you did. I thank you for all that you taught me. You made this book so much better!

To my colleague, Ms. Amber Williams: your feedback and encouragement helped me to understand the value of this project. I appreciate you taking the time to help me.

To my "work wife", Mrs. Nashon Williams, thank you for your insights and for challenging me to do more. It's coming. I miss you.

Finally, I could never express enough gratitude to Mr. Ernest Donelson II. Thank you for insisting on helping me and for intuitively "getting" a vision I couldn't fully articulate.

Introduction

When you think of black Americans and their fight for equal rights, you probably think of Dr. Martin Luther King, Jr. He is one of the most famous people in history and one of only two American to have a national holiday named in their honor. From 1955 until his death in 1968, Dr. King gave speeches, led protests, and wrote books to bring attention to the unfair treatment of black people in the United States.

Public Domain Image

It's important to remember that Dr. King was not the first person in this country to fight back against racism. Since the first black Americans were enslaved here, there have been men and women who fought for freedom. And every new freedom fighter is influenced by those who came before them.

One of Martin Luther King's role models was a man named Dr. Vernon Johns.

Johns was an important guide and example to Dr. King and the other religious leaders who shaped the Civil Rights Movement of the 1950s and 60s.

Vernon Johns was a preacher, an educator, and an **activist**. He often shocked people because he challenged them to think differently. He knew that equality for black people meant more than changing the minds of white people. It meant more than changing laws. Black people would have to change the way they thought and acted, as well. Johns pointed out that white people were not the only ones who sometimes saw black people as **inferior**; many black people saw themselves that way, too.

People were troubled by the idea that black Americans—especially those with money, **social status**, and education—must change themselves before they could expect others to

activist-a person who brings others together to fight for a cause or to fight for their rights

inferior- less than other people

social status- a high place in the community

change. They thought that Johns was crazy and that his ideas were dangerous. Dr. Johns ignored their criticisms.

Though he was a church leader, he openly rejected common ideas about how a church leader should speak and act in public. Instead of being proper and **dignified**, Johns focused on promoting **economic freedom** and fighting against racism.

From 1948 to 1952, Vernon Johns was the pastor of Dexter Avenue Baptist Church in Montgomery, Alabama. Three years after he left, Martin Luther King, Jr. was hired to take over as leader of that church. King was only 25 years old when he was hired, and he had

Public Domain Image

never been the pastor of his own church before.

Many believe Dexter Avenue Baptist Church and the city of Montgomery wouldn't have accepted Dr. King if Vernon Johns hadn't been there first, that Dr. Johns prepared people for the ideas of Dr. King. Often called the "Father of the Civil Rights Movement", Johns was an advisor to Dr. King and many other future leaders. Although most people have never heard of him, the impact of Vernon Johns as a **thought leader** is still felt today.

dignified- having a lot of pride, requiring respect

economic freedom- having no need for money from others

thought leader- a person whose ideas influence others; an influencer

1

Challenging Beginnings

Vernon Napolean Johns was born on April 22, 1892, in Darlington Heights, Virginia. Darlington Heights was and still is a **rural** community outside of the larger town of Farmville. Vernon was born only 27 years after the Civil War forced an end to **chattel slavery** in the United States.

> **rural-** describes a community that is less populated, often a farming community

> **chattel slavery-** a system of slavery in which the enslaved are forced to work without pay and have no human rights

Vernon's Mother

Vernon's mother was Sallie Branch Price Johns. Sallie was born during slavery. She was the child of an enslaved woman and a white landowner named Thomas Price. During slavery, it was common for landowners to have children with the black women they enslaved.

Thomas Price, Sallie's father, killed another white man for trying to attack Sallie's mother. It was rare at the time for a white person to protect a black person from another white person.

A judge sentenced Thomas Price to death for the murder, but the governor is the political leader of the state and has the right to change a judge's decision. The governor of Virginia decided that Thomas Price would spend the rest of his life in prison instead. So Vernon Johns' white grandfather lived the rest of his days in the Virginia State **Penitentiary** for protecting the enslaved mother of his child.

Sallie's mother died when Sallie was still a girl. With her father in prison, she was left in the care of his wife. No one ever admitted that Thomas Price was Sallie's father, or called his wife her stepmother. Rather, people pretended that Mrs. "Kitty" Price had taken Sallie in as an orphan, just the child of an enslaved woman who died on her land. At that time, few white men ever claimed mixed-race children as their own. Many kept their own children enslaved. Sallie

penitentiary- a large prison

was enslaved as a child, but she was allowed to live in the house with her father's wife and was likely treated better than some other enslaved people.

Vernon's Father

Vernon's father was Willie Johns. Willie's parents, Vernon's grandparents, were both born enslaved. After slavery ended, Willie's father, Monroe Johns, worked as a shoemaker. Monroe was accused of killing the white man who owned the land where he lived and worked. There was no trial, no judge, and no governor to save his life. His guilt was assumed, and he was hanged as punishment.

No one knows how Vernon Johns felt about the fact that both of his grandfathers had been punished for murders. But, surely, he was aware of the differences in their treatment. His white grandfather was sent to prison for his crime. His black grandfather was hanged without even a trial.

Despite what happened to his father, and maybe because of it, Willie Johns became a very **industrious** man. He was both a farmer and a Baptist minister. For years he traveled as a preacher, visiting churches and receiving small payments for preaching his sermons. Finally, he built his own small church on his land in Darlington Heights, where he tended his farm and raised his family.

industrious- hard working and careful

Early Years

Vernon was the second of seven children born to Willie and Sallie Johns. He had one older sister, a younger sister, and four younger brothers. The Johns family was poor but self-sufficient. They depended on the animals they raised and the crops they grew to keep food on the table. As the oldest son, Vernon grew up farming alongside his dad.

When Vernon was five, he and his older sister started going to a one-room school four miles away from their house. In one-room schools, students of all ages shared the same classroom. One teacher taught all of the students, and the older children helped to teach the younger children. From the beginning, Vernon loved to read and did an excellent job on his lessons. His teachers soon realized that he had a remarkable memory.

Photo Credit: Library of Congress

When Vernon was 10, he and his sister went away to

school at the Boydton Academic and Bible Institute, forty-five miles away from Darlington Heights. The Boydton Institute was a Christian school, started by the **Freedmen's Bureau** to educate the formerly enslaved and their children. It was outside of Boydton, Virginia on the abandoned campus of a Methodist college that had closed down. Part of Boydton Institute's goal was to train black people to become preachers and teachers.

Vernon enjoyed Boydton and wanted to stay there until he was ready for college. Sadly, his father died when he was only 15 years old. As the oldest son, his mother needed him home to work the farm and support his family.

The Boydton Institute
Photo Credit: Southern Virginia Homefront

Even though he went on to become a church leader, an accomplished educator, and a pioneer social activist, Vernon Johns would hold on to his family's farm for the rest of his life.

> **The Freedmen's Bureau**- a government organization created to help formerly enslaved people after they were freed

2

Back to School

Despite having to leave school for a while, Vernon didn't give up on his education. He was already a farmer like his father had been, and wanted to follow in his father's footsteps as a preacher, too.

In 1911, at the age of 19, Vernon enrolled in Virginia Union University for one year. This was the beginning of a lifelong connection to historically black colleges and universities (HBCUs). Like Boydton, these schools were created to help newly freed black people develop the skills they needed to be successful as free citizens. While he was at Virginia Union, Johns worked on the school's farm to help pay his fees.

He then went on to Virginia Theological Seminary and College. A seminary is a school where people are trained to be religious leaders. Johns did not last long at Virginia Theological Seminary, though. He got expelled. Rumor has

it that he was accused of cheating on a written assignment–
he was naturally very good with words– and punched one
of his accusers.

Soon after, he was accepted to Oberlin College in Ohio.

Oberlin College has a unique history. Unlike most colleges at the time, Oberlin admitted both men and women
when it opened in 1833. Two years later they began admit-
ting black students during a time when most black people
in the United States were still enslaved. Oberlin was the
first college in America to welcome all students, no matter
their race or gender.

Oberlin was founded by men who also fought to bring
an end to chattel slavery, and the campus had been a stop
on the **Underground Railroad**. Runaways- this is what
they called enslaved people who freed themselves– used
Oberlin as a hiding place as they traveled further north.
Many headed to Canada to avoid being caught and returned
to enslavement.

> **Underground Railroad**- a network
> of people who helped black people escape
> enslavement. They set up secret routes and
> kept people safe as they traveled north.

Public Domain Image

Vernon Johns thrived at Oberlin. He became a student minister at a local church and won awards for his exceptional sermons. Rising to the top of his class, he earned his **Divinity** degree and was **ordained** as a Baptist minister in 1918.

The Chicago Race Riot

Reverend Johns went on to study **Theology** in graduate school at the University of Chicago. A graduate school offers additional training for people who already have college degrees. Johns was still enrolled there during the summer of 1919. That summer is infamous in the history of Chicago and across the country.

Divinity- the study of God and religion

ordained- (religious) officially recognized

Theology- the study of the Bible

Racial tension was growing. Many black people had migrated to Chicago for factory jobs, and to avoid violence in the South. Recent **immigrants** from Europe had also come to Chicago looking for a better life. The two groups competed over jobs and housing.

Most of the public facilities in Chicago were **integrated**, but not the beaches that lined Lake Michigan. In July 1919, a young black man named Eugene Williams swam onto a white beach. It's not clear whether he did it on purpose, or he just wasn't paying attention to where he was going. And he never made it back to the shore to tell his side of the story.

> **immigrants**- a person who comes to live in a new country
>
> **integrated**- open to people of different races

According to witnesses, a group of white men attacked Williams, battering him with rocks until he drowned in the lake. But none of them were arrested. Instead, police arrested a black man, even though witnesses told them the man didn't have anything to do with the killing.

What happened next was a week of violent fighting between black people and white people on Chicago's south side. White rioters set fire to over 100 homes in hopes of forcing black folks to leave the city. The riots were brought under control after the **National Guard** was called in to bring order.

Twenty-three black people and fifteen white people were killed. Over 500 people, two-thirds of them black, were hurt during the week of chaos. The Chicago Police Department was criticized for arresting more black rioters than white, even though white rioters had committed most of the **arson** and other violent acts.

Chicago Police tried to get the riot under control.
Public Domain Image

The National Guard- a branch of the military that responds to emergencies in the states

arson- a fire set on purpose

Across America, the Summer of 1919 is known as "Red Summer". There were similar race riots in over 20 cities. In rural Arkansas, for instance, over 100 black people were killed during a riot that lasted only two days. Many believe that Red Summer was caused by the job shortage that followed the end of **World War I**. Once the soldiers returned home, there were simply more workers than there was work.

Vernon Johns remained in Chicago for a year after the riots, and then returned to a familiar place.

> **World War I**- a war that involved the U.S. and most European nations, 1914-1918.

3

Making Moves

Having been kicked out as a problem student years before, Vernon Johns returned to Virginia Theological Seminary as a teacher in 1920. He also became the pastor of Court Street Baptist Church. The two roles went hand in hand.

Court Street Baptist is the oldest black Baptist church in Lynchburg, Virginia. It was started by formerly enslaved people and was built near the site where they worshipped while in bondage. Court Street Baptist is still the tallest building in downtown Lynchburg and appears on the National Registry of Historic Places, the official list of places that are valuable to American culture and need to be preserved.

The link between Virginia Theological Seminary and Court Street Baptist goes back to 1886. The seminary was founded by Court Street pastor Dr. Phillip Morris, who oversaw the building of the seminary and was also its first president. He continued to lead the church at the same time.

For Dr. Johns, this stay in Virginia lasted for 6 years. It is not entirely clear why he left Lynchburg in 1926. Some say the church fired him because he traveled too much. Others say he made some **controversial** comments and brought negative attention to the church. Either way, leaving Court Street Baptist

Virginia Theological Seminary
Public Domain Image

also meant leaving Virginia Theological Seminary for a second time.

This time, he was headed to a place where black voices were demanding to be heard, putting black culture on display in ways America had never seen.

> **controversial**- causing upset among people

The New Negro

Harlem is a neighborhood in New York City. It's best known as the backdrop of the Harlem Renaissance, also called the "New Negro Movement." In the 1920s and 30s, Harlem was home to many of the most influential writers, artists, and performers in the country. Even today, the

Harlem Renaissance is identified as the height of artistic expression for black Americans.

These "New Negroes" were letting the world know what it meant to be black in America. They wrote about it, sang, danced, painted, and made sculptures. They performed plays and published essays. Their work did not apologize for its blackness. Instead, it commanded attention and respect. And the world took notice.

As Director of the Baptist Educational Center in Harlem, Dr. Johns was a religious leader, seemingly disconnected from Harlem's arts community. Still, the focus on black self-expression fueled his work there. Under Johns' leadership, Baptist Educational Center overflowed with groundbreaking approaches to church leadership.

Johns hosted weekly gatherings of pastors who had begun to speak out against **discrimination**. Guest speakers included religious leaders–college presidents and deans, prominent pastors, and Theology educators– from across America and as far away as London, England. Johns published many of their ideas in a small journal called "Negro Pulpit Opinion: An Interpretation of Christianity by Colored People." Like the Harlem Renaissance artists, he was highlighting the idea that black people- commonly called "negro" and "colored" at that time– had something unique to say.

discrimination- unfair treatment of a group or groups

A New Beginning

In 1927, Johns left Harlem and returned to Virginia. Later that year, he married a beautiful, educated woman named Altona Trent. Altona didn't come from a poor farming family like Vernon's. Her father was the president of an HBCU, Livingstone College in North Carolina.

A Collection of Children's Songs by Altona Trent Johns

Photo Credit: New York Public Library

Ms. Trent had two college degrees; she was an accomplished classical pianist and a music teacher. She wrote books that other musicians used for lessons and performances. Vernon and Altona Johns had three daughters and three sons together. They would remain married for 38 years until Vernon's death in 1965.

West Virginia

The newlyweds moved to West Virginia, where Vernon took over as pastor of First Baptist Church in Charleston. While in West Virginia, he started a company called Farm and City Enterprises. As the name suggests, Farm and City aimed to build relationships between black people who were still working the land and those who had moved to the cities for factory work. His goal was to help black farmers make more money for their crops and to keep the city folks connected to their roots.

Johns believed strongly that black people should continue to use **agriculture** to make money. During one of his sermons at First Baptist, he announced that he was setting up a fish business. This was an odd activity for the pastor of a large church!

Many of his church members disagreed with the move. Dr. Johns was an important man, a leader, and he should act like one. But Dr. Johns ignored them and went ahead with his plan. According to him, he got 40 phone calls about fish for every one call he got about religion.

Dr. Johns promoted self-sufficiency. He believed that to overcome poverty, all black people should run some kind of small business. That way they could always make money that didn't depend on working for others.

agriculture- using nature to produce food: growing crops, raising animals, and fishing

4

Three Strikes, You're Out!

In 1929, Johns returned to Virginia Theological Seminary for the third time. After being kicked out as a student and possibly fired as a teacher, he was now taking over as president of the college.

The school was having **financial** problems, and people were afraid it might have to close. As president, Johns worked hard to raise the needed money. By now he was very popular as a public speaker, so he spent a lot of his time traveling around the South giving speeches at churches and colleges.

financial- related to money

He used every opportunity to request donations for Virginia Theological Seminary. Johns's fundraising efforts were aggressive. In addition to giving speeches, he set up fundraising events in Virginia and Washington, D.C. The owner of a local bank helped him to organize a special **campaign** that would appeal especially to white **donors**. Before long, the **Board of Trustees** was amazed at how quickly the school's financial situation improved.

True to his roots, Johns bought a farm near the campus. Students who didn't have money to pay their fees were allowed to work on the farm to earn what they needed. The farm also provided food for the College's students and faculty.

Even though he'd raised a lot of money to help Virginia Theological Seminary, Johns' temper soon got in the way. Some students felt like he mistreated them. They accused him of yelling and using harsh words when they disagreed with the way he did things. Student leaders claimed he didn't take enough time to listen to their opinions and ideas.

campaign-a plan to raise money

donors- people who give money

Board of Trustees- leaders trusted to guide an institution

In 1933, students began protesting at a number of historically black colleges and universities. Virginia Theological Seminary students held a meeting in the college chapel to talk about staging a **strike** of their own. They decided to issue a list of demands to the college and to call for Johns' dismissal as president. Their complaints included Johns' forcing students to work long hours on the farm, his rude treatment of them, and his use of classroom space to raise chickens.

When their demands weren't met, the students chose to go on strike. They refused to attend classes and demanded that Johns be fired immediately. Many of them carried signs that said "If Johns Stays, We Leave." To make matters worse, President Johns clashed with a student at a protest and then demanded that the student be arrested.

The teachers were complaining about Dr. Johns's leadership, too. They wanted the college to be more traditional– no chickens in classrooms, for example– and they worried that the college's money problems had not been completely solved. Some claimed that Johns had forced them to join his company, Farm and City Enterprises.

strike- a refusal to work or participate

In the face of so much backlash, Dr. Johns chose to submit his **resignation**. He joked publicly about being kicked out of the same school three times. This time he would not return.

resignation- a letter written to quit a job

5

Harder Times

The Great Depression, from 1929 to 1942, was a very difficult time in America. Many people were out of work. There were few jobs, and it was almost impossible for most Americans to make enough money. All over the country, people were poorer than they had ever been.

The Great Depression made hard times even harder for black Americans. With so many families struggling, black farmers could no longer sell their crops or could only sell them at very low prices. Few could make enough money to take care of their families.

In cities, there were some jobs that had always been done by black workers. Collecting garbage, operating elevators, cooking, and cleaning houses had always been thought of as "negro jobs." But during the Great Depression, for the sake of survival, many white Americans took these jobs that they would have never taken in earlier years. There were even cases where white mobs killed black workers for taking jobs that they wanted.

Hungry Americans waiting in line for free food
during the Great Depression.
Public Domain Image

The Farm Movement

During this time, Vernon Johns supported the "Back to the Farm" movement. The movement highlighted the downsides of city living and encouraged people to return to farming to support their families.

After being forced to leave Virginia Theological Seminary yet again, Johns returned home to work on his own farm. He is quoted as saying, "This is where the forest grows night and day to feed the poor man's fire and build the shelter for his children." Johns tried to teach people that they could get what they needed to survive if they knew how to work the land. They could build their own homes and furniture, grow food, and provide for their families without having a paycheck from a job.

Dr. Johns believed in working hard and having a lot of different skills. He used his mind to make money as a preacher and an educator. He used his hands to fish, grow crops, and raise livestock. Wherever he went, he found ways to make money off the land.

6

Deeper South

It's important to remember that Vernon Johns was born less than 30 years after the end of the Civil War and the end of chattel slavery. America was still trying to rebuild itself. And it had a lot of rebuilding to do!

Almost all Civil War battles were fought in the South. Farms, stores, and sometimes whole towns were destroyed. The South also needed to build an economy that didn't rely on free labor. Landowners had been making money from the work of enslaved people for 246 years, but it wasn't legal to do this anymore.

The Civil War was fought because the southern states tried to break away and make their own country. The purpose of the war was to keep the country together. The North won and the South stayed. But the challenge was how to move forward as a united country after people had been shooting at each other for four years.

And America had to figure out what to do with her newest citizens. The end of the Civil War meant freedom for over 100,00 people enslaved in the South. After freedom came the right to citizenship. And, after that, the right to vote.

During Reconstruction, black Americans gained political power in southern states for the first time. With this power, they elected black lawmakers and public officials. This was new, and a lot of people didn't like it. President Andrew Johnson sent soldiers to the South, trying to protect **freedmen** from violence.

But by 1877, Reconstruction was over, the Union soldiers left, and many of the rights given to freedmen were quickly taken away.

The Southern states adopted laws known as **Jim Crow laws**. These laws were meant to keep black people as second-class citizens. They kept black and white people separate in all public places. This is called segregation and, in many cities, it lasted for over 100 years.

> **freedmen**- people who used to be enslaved

> **Jim Crow Laws**- Jim Crow was a character who made black people look lazy and mean. He was used as a symbol of segregation.

Public Domain Image

In segregated cities, black and white people did not live in the same neighborhoods or go to the same schools. Black riders had to ride in the back of city buses while white riders rode in the front. Many businesses would not serve black customers or made them stand outside to wait for service. Companies kept their black and white employees separate if they hired black people at all, and they paid black workers less for doing the same jobs.

In most public places, black people were required to follow special rules: use the back door, sit only in the "colored" section, and use the "colored" restrooms and water fountains. When they went shopping, black customers could not try on clothes or shoes. Many hotels and restaurants turned them away altogether.

Public Domain Image

Southern states also found ways to take away black people's right to vote. This meant that they had no influence on who would become mayor, sheriff, congressman, or governor. Only white citizens were allowed to choose the leaders who made the laws, so the laws were made to benefit white citizens.

Jim Crow laws existed across the south but were strictest in the "deep south" states of Mississippi, Alabama, Florida, Georgia, and South Carolina. So this was the way of things when Dr. Johns arrived in Montgomery, Alabama in 1948.

To Alabama and Dexter Avenue

Vernon Johns was known for speaking out against racial inequality. He didn't sugarcoat his words or avoid even the most difficult topics. He also didn't let his family participate in any segregated activities.

According to Dr. Johns, Black people were unwise for spending money at white businesses where they were treated poorly. He told black people that they should own their own businesses, and should support one another's businesses so that more money would stay in the black communities.

Segregation did lead to the financial success of some black people in the South. Because segregation limited the choices of black **consumers**, they often went to black-owned stores and restaurants. They used services— doctors, repairmen, even funeral homes—owned by black families. This created a thriving black middle-class in many segregated cities.

consumers- people who buy things

In Montgomery, Alabama many of the successful black folks attended Dexter Avenue Baptist Church downtown. The church was established in 1877. It's s only a few short blocks from the state's capitol building and was well-known around the city. White leaders pointed to the wealth and success of folks at Dexter Avenue Baptist as an example that black people could have good lives in the segregated South.

Public Domain Image

In 1948, Vernon Johns became the pastor of Dexter Avenue Baptist.

Johns believed that even though some black people had money, they were still hurt by racial discrimination. They were subjected to constant disrespect, and they couldn't do all the things white people could. They couldn't live wherever they wanted or send their kids to any school they chose, no matter how much money they had. He pressured the folks at Dexter Avenue Baptist to use their influence to fight back against Jim Crow laws that denied them equal treatment.

According to Dr. Johns, many of the people at Dexter Avenue Baptist were too concerned with social status and not concerned enough with making a difference. Because they had money, he argued that they were in the best position to make things better. Instead of looking down on others who had less than them, they should help other black people to improve their lives.

Vernon Johns was more concerned with progress than he was with appearances. He was the same pastor that had run a successful fish business in West Virginia and raised chickens in college classrooms. Now in Montgomery, he was once again faced with a congregation that wanted him to dress up and act important. Dexter Avenue was an important church full of important people, and they wanted their pastor to look and act the part.

Dr. Johns rejected all of this. While living in Montgomery, he continued to farm. He sometimes dressed in overalls and a farmer's hat and boots and set up a farmstand in front of the church. He was a troublemaker. On purpose.

pic farmstand

Years before the Montgomery Bus Boycott, Dr. Johns refused to ride segregated buses and once demanded his money back when he was directed to the back of a city bus. He also made a stir by ordering food at a white-only lunch counter. Johns was trying to get the attention of black folks in Montgomery. He was trying to show them what it meant to stand up for themselves.

His actions upset folks, but Dr. Johns was known for being an exciting preacher. His deep voice easily filled a room, and his sermons were unique and creative. Most folks had never heard preaching like his. Sure, he used the Bible as all preachers did, but he often mixed in well-known literature and poetry. He could quote all kinds of books without looking at them, and he didn't use any notes. People loved to hear him preach!

Decades before the Black Lives Matter movement, Dr. Vernon Johns was using his pulpit to speak out against police brutality. He raged against a legal system that failed to punish the police or private citizens when they killed black people. "It's Safe to Murder Negroes in Montgomery". This was the title of one of Johns's most controversial sermons. He talked openly about racial hatred, and he didn't seem to care if he made white people angry. He was fearless! And this scared a lot of black folks, especially the members of Dexter Avenue Baptist. In the South, angry white people often meant church burnings and other acts of violence.

But Dr. Johns didn't only call out racists. He also believed in speaking out against black people for wrongdoing. He publicly condemned a member of the congregation who was allowed to go free after murdering his own wife. And he refused to say nice things at the funeral of another man, because he wasn't really a good person, and Dr. Johns wasn't going to pretend that he was.

Dr. Johns claimed he had a vision for the people at Dexter Avenue Baptist. Many of them were educated, and he thought that he could teach them to do things differently. There are stories that he interrupted weddings and other important events to announce items he had for sale. He was seen around the community selling various things, and even driving a watermelon truck.

Dr. Johns was trying to make a point. He thought black people were too focused on fancy clothes and nice cars. They needed to build their own small businesses, not just buy things all the time.

Pastor Johns eventually became discouraged. He tried to quit his job at Dexter Avenue Baptist four times, but each time the church refused to accept his resignation.

By 1952, Johns felt sure he couldn't reach the members at Dexter Avenue. He thought they would never stand up for their community, and he knew he would never behave the way they thought a pastor should. Like the students at Virginia Theological Seminary, they accused him of having a bad temper and lashing out at those who disagreed with him. Johns submitted his resignation for the 5th time. This time, the church accepted.

Vernon's wife Altona was teaching at Alabama State College (now Alabama State University), a historically black college in Montgomery. When Vernon lost his job at the church, she immediately resigned her position and accepted a job at a college in Virginia. She left Montgomery right away, thinking her husband would soon follow.

Vernon, shocked that the church had accepted his resignation, hesitated to leave Montgomery. He continued to live in the house provided by Dexter Avenue Baptist, even though he no longer worked for the church. Finally, the church leaders had the heat and lights turned off in the house. Johns returned once again to his family farm.

Dr. Johns & Dr. King

By 1954, Dexter Avenue Baptist Church was still looking for another pastor. When churches are hiring, they invite available preachers to give guest sermons, so they can meet them and see if they are any good. Two years after Dr. Johns left, Martin Luther King, Jr., a young preacher from Atlanta, was invited to Dexter Avenue Baptist.

Ralph Abernathy, a young minister in Montgomery, was a friend of the King family. He invited young Martin to his home the night before his guest sermon. Vernon Johns was one of Abernathy's **mentors**.

mentor-a personal or professional guide

Rev. Ralph
Abernathy
*Public Domain
Image*

Vernon Johns was scheduled to speak at another church in Montgomery on the same Sunday that Martin Luther King would be visiting Dexter Avenue Baptist. He was asked to have dinner at the Abernathy home on the same night.

Dr. Johns knew Martin Luther King, Sr.; they had both been Baptist preachers for many years. He reached out to the elder King to propose a travel arrangement. He wanted to leave his home in Virginia and meet young Dr. King at his family home in Atlanta. Then the two of them would ride together to Montgomery, over two hours away, so they could have some time to talk.

Once they arrived at the Abernathy home, the three men talked about Montgomery, civil rights, and Dexter Avenue Baptist church. Johns jokingly warned King about the folks at the church being stuck in their ways and told him who was likely to give him a hard time. Dr. Johns felt sure that Martin would get the job at Dexter Avenue Baptist. He was the son of a respected Atlanta preacher, charming, and only 25 years old. The folks at Dexter Avenue would not expect him to make any trouble.

Martin delivered his guest sermon the next day. The church offered him a job as their full-time pastor, and he accepted.

Dr. Johns continued to visit Montgomery regularly. He and Dr. King continued to visit the Abernathy home together.

The Montgomery Bus Boycott started the following year. Just a few weeks into the citywide protest, Dr. Johns went with Dr. King to meet with city leaders. Dr. King was seen as the boycott's leader, and the city wanted to negotiate a way to bring the protest to an end.

In 1956, Martin Luther King wrote a book about the Montgomery Bus Boycott, called *Stride Toward Freedom: The Montgomery Story.* He made it clear that he respected and admired the man who had come before him at Dexter Avenue Baptist:

> Vernon Johns was a brilliant preacher with a creative mind and an incredibly retentive memory. A fearless man, he never allowed an injustice to come to his attention without speaking out against it...He often chided the congregation for sitting up so proudly with their many academic degrees, and yet lacking the very thing that the degrees should confer, that is, self-respect.

Marting Luther King understood what Vernon Johns had been trying to do at Dexter Avenue Baptist. He was trying to help the people to find their self-respect so that they would stop accepting disrespect from others. He, in fact, had followed Dr. Johns' lead and made Dexter Avenue Baptist a key location in the fight for racial justice.

Dreamers and Mountaintops

Martin Luther King became famous for leading the bus boycott, and later leading huge protest marches. He captured the nation's attention because he had a special way with words. His manner of speaking was bold and colorful, a southern accent hanging just around the edges of his voice. King's most famous speech was the "I Have a Dream" speech, given at the 1963 March on Washington for Jobs and Freedom.

Religious historians say that "I Have a Dream" was very similar to an earlier sermon given by Vernon Johns entitled "Along Came the Dreamer". Johns never expressed anger about King borrowing his ideas. It was normal for ministers to do this. Years later, however, family members claimed that he was very sad about not being invited to participate in The March on Washington.

Dreams and dreamers weren't the only themes shared by the two preachers. On the night before he was killed, Martin Luther King gave a powerful speech that many call his "mountaintop" speech:

> I've been to the mountaintop... I just want to do God's will. And He's allowed me to go up to the mountaintop. And I've looked over. And I've seen the Promised Land. I may not get there with you.

But I want you to know tonight, that we, as a people, will get to the Promised Land!

Many believe this speech was also inspired by a Vernon Johns sermon. In a sermon called "Transfigured Moments", given at Court Street Baptist Church, Vernon Johns spoke of mountaintop experiences years earlier:

It is good to be the possessor of some mountain-top experience. Not to know life on the heights, is to suffer an impoverishing incompleteness. To be sure, there is better opportunity for practical pursuits in the valley regions, and life is easier and safer there: but views are possible from the mountain top which are not to be had in the vale. A missionary in the Balkans once took a small boy, who lived at the base of a mountain, on a journey up its side. When they gained the summit, the little climber looked this way and that, and then said with astonishment: "My! What a wonderful world! I never dreamed it was so large." Horizons broaden when we stand on the heights. There is always the danger that we will make of life too much of a dead-level existence: that we will make of life a slavish following of the water courses; a monotonous tread of beaten paths; a matter of absorbing, spiritless, deadening routine. There is the danger that we will drop our lives into the passing current to be kept steadily going, we hardly know where or why... From some mountain eminence let us have occasionally a quiet look upon life, to reflect what it means and whither it is carrying us. The luminaries of humanity were familiar with elevated ground.

Both men used the "mountaintop" as a **metaphor** for a highly religious experience. Dr. Johns discussed it as a goal to be reached. Going to the mountaintop allowed a person to live a fuller life. It was the highest height of human existence, an experience that changed you forever. Seemingly in response, Dr. King said that he had made it to the mountaintop. From there, he could see the "promised land" where black people would have all of the rights and privileges promised to them as American citizens. Dr. King gave his speech three years after the death of Dr. Johns, on the night before he was assassinated.

The last known contact between the two men was in 1963, about one month after the March on Washington for Jobs & Freedom. On September 15, 1963, four young girls were killed in a church bombing in Birmingham, Alabama.

metaphor- a comparison between things that seems unalike

Dr. King was called on to deliver a **eulogy** at the funeral of three of the girls. He accepted the invitation but struggled to find the words to clearly communicate the mixture of anger, sadness, and hopefulness appropriate for the occasion.

Dr. King sent his lawyer, Mr. Chauncey Eskridge to Virginia to find Vernon Johns. He hoped Dr. Johns would share his sermon notebooks, to help King come up with the right words for the little girls' eulogy. Eskridge found Johns at the store he owned in Petersburg, Virginia, and explained why he had come. Johns didn't give him any notebooks, though. Some say this is because he was still using his notes for guest sermons and speaking engagements. Others claim that he never had any because he was known to memorize his sermons and was seldom seen looking at any notes. Whatever the reason, Mr. Eskridge left Virginia empty-handed.

> **eulogy**-a speech given about a person during their funeral

8

"The Romance of
Death"

After leaving Montgomery, Vernon Johns lived in Petersburg, Virginia with his wife and traveled back and forth to
his farm in Darlington Heights.

From 1955 to 1960, he served as director of Maryland
Baptist Center and School of Religion in Baltimore, Maryland. The center provided training to black preachers. He
also continued his work with Farm and City Enterprises
and organized a co-op supermarket. In a co-op, the store is
owned by the customers. This gave farmers the opportunity
to sell their goods directly to consumers.

The store Dr. Johns owned was in one of Petersburg's
poorer neighborhoods. Two nights a week, he would give
sermons in the store. Because it was a "bad" neighborhood,

his listeners were often people you would never find in a traditional church setting.

The store was broken into twice. Although he was an older man now, Dr. Johns still wasn't one to show fear. He started sleeping at the store because he wanted to catch the thieves himself. Before long, they struck again. By the time the police made it to the store that night, there were two burglars unconscious on the floor. Vernon Johns, at age 70, had knocked both of them out cold.

Vernon Johns's daughter, Jeanne, later said that this was just an example of her father being himself. No matter his age, Vernon Johns refused to stand by and let others take advantage of him.

Dr. Johns still gave guest sermons at churches and spoke at colleges. Many colleges had an annual "Week of Prayer" and he was often invited to lead these events.

In early 1965, Dr. Johns agreed to join the faculty of Howard University for the upcoming school year. Howard is a historically black university in Washington D.C. The largest HBCU in the country, many black people call it "The Mecca." Johns had been a guest speaker there many times before, and Howard's former president had helped him when he was raising money for Virginia Theological Seminary.

In June of 1965 he gave a sermon called "The Romance of Death" on the Howard University campus. Ten days later, he passed away in Washington D.C. Dr. Johns is buried in the place he loved most, on his family farm in Darlington Heights. In 1994, the state of Virginia erected a historic marker there in his honor.

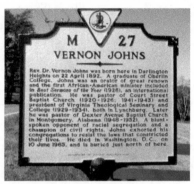

Source: The Historical Marker Database

9

Legacy

During his life, Vernon Johns made a lot of people uncomfortable. Some say he simply told too much truth. He refused to say or do things that he didn't believe in, even if it would make other people feel better. Dr. Johns challenged people to think differently about what it meant to be free. He challenged them to let go of their fears so they could hold onto their self-respect. He wanted black people to work together, and he was impatient with those who didn't fight back against injustice.

Vernon Johns called on black people in America to take financial responsibility for their own lives and to financially support their own community. Johns emphasized each individual's responsibility for their own freedom. He insisted that if black people wanted to change America, they would first have to change themselves.

He also openly criticized white Christian leaders for only

focusing on Jesus as a forgiving figure who paid for everyone's sins. He is quoted as saying, "I want to talk about Jesus before the cross!" He wanted to talk about the Jesus who stood up for the poor and the weak. According to Dr. Johns, white preachers ignored this part of the Bible because it made white people look bad for either **oppressing** others or failing to protect the oppressed.

Vernon Johns was a preacher, an educator, an entrepreneur, a farmer, a father, and a husband. Though he was never rich and was only well-known in religious circles, his influence went beyond churches and church leaders.

oppress- to keep in hardship, subject to injustice

Barbara Johns

Vernon Johns' niece, Barbara Johns, became an important part of the early Civil Rights Movement when she was still a teenager. Barbara was influenced by her uncle to learn the history of black people in America, and to fight back against racism and discrimination.

In 1951, when she was only sixteen, Barbara organized a student strike at Robert R. Moton High School in Farmville, Virginia. Moton was Farmville's all-black high school. It was overcrowded and poorly heated. The roof leaked so badly that students sometimes used umbrellas inside their classrooms. Barbara led Moton students on a march to the county courthouse to protest conditions in the segregated school.

Later, she and other students contacted the NAACP and

filed a lawsuit against the school board for failing to address the problems. Their lawsuit became a part of the *Brown v. Board of Education* case that went to the Supreme Court. The Supreme Court is the highest court in the country. All 50 states have to follow whatever they decided. In *Brown v. Board of Education,* the court decided that segregated schools were not legal.   This case is the reason that all children can go to school together, no matter what color they are.

After the lawsuit, Barbara's parents worried about her safety. She had shown remarkable courage and leadership, but black activists often faced threats of violence. They sent her to live with Vernon and Altona Johns and their children.

Left Out

Historians believe that Barbara Johns' role in the Civil Rights Movement has not gotten much attention because she was a teenager when she led the student strike at Moton High. Today, a beautiful bronze statue in front of the Virginia state capitol building honors Barbara and her schoolmates. She is also the title of a book called *The Girl from the Tar Paper School.*

Source: The United States Civil Rights Trail

Like his niece, Vernon Johns's role in the fight for racial justice has largely been ignored. Some believe that this is because he did not actively participate in what we call the Civil Rights Movement. So why didn't he?

Dr. Johns was an important example for the pastors that went on to lead the Civil Rights Movement. He didn't only preach about religion, but also used his pulpit to highlight social and political issues. He called people to action. He made equal rights and social justice the business of the black church.

Still, it would have likely been impossible for Dr. Johns to participate in the nonviolent protests led by Martin Luther King. Dr. Johns never embraced nonviolence. In fact, he celebrated the stories of abolitionists who had used violence to fight back against slavery. Civil rights leaders were sometimes physically attacked. Martin Luther King was pushed, stabbed, and hit in the head with rocks. Johns was known for having a terrible temper, and he surely would have never tolerated such treatment. The way he handled the burglars who broke into his store is clear evidence that he was willing to use violence when he thought it was necessary.

Many of the Civil Rights protests of the 1950s and 1960s were focused on achieving **integration**. Dr. Johns never promoted this idea. Rather, he highlighted what black people needed to do for themselves: the more educated should help the less educated; urban blacks should support rural blacks, and every man must help himself. Even though he had white relatives and worked alongside white people at times, there is no evidence that Vernon Johns thought integration was the answer to black Americans' problems.

Vernon Johns is often called the "Father of the Civil Rights Movement" because his actions and ideas inspired the men and women that shaped that movement. Still, he remained on the outside. Some historians claim that he even criticized movement leaders for being too fearful to really stand up for their rights. He simply did not agree with the message that black people should accept violence and not fight back.

integration- the inclusion of people of all races

Brought to Light
Although his name doesn't appear in History books, Dr. Vernon Johns' life and work have not been completely

overlooked. In 1988, author Taylor Branch published the book *Parting the Waters: America in the King Years*. This book introduced many people to the work of Dr. Johns. Still more people learned about Johns from a 1994 television movie called *The Road to Freedom: The Vernon Johns Story*. One of the producers of the movie was basketball **legend** Kareem Abdul-Jabar.

There is a historical marker honoring Dr. Johns on the site of his family farm in Darlington Heights, Virginia. In nearby Petersburg, an elementary school was re-named Vernon Johns Jr. High in 2009; it is now Vernon Johns Middle School. A middle school on the south side of Chicago, Vernon Johns Community Academy, closed in 2008.

legend- a very famous person

Conclusion

A person's legacy is what they leave behind in the world after they're gone. Vernon Johns is quoted as saying, "You should be ashamed to die until you've made some contribution to mankind." His contributions were made in words and actions. At a time when many black Americans lived their lives in fear, Dr. Vernon Johns appeared fearless.

Dr. Johns believed that he deserved freedom and that he was responsible for keeping himself free. He didn't shut up, and he didn't back down. His freedom cost him plenty. Despite his brilliant mind and visionary leadership, he was repeatedly fired from his jobs. And, in his later years, he was excluded from a movement that he had helped to inspire.

Whether or not people agreed with Vernon Johns' methods—like trying to sell vegetables during church services—it is impossible to deny his bravery. He was different, he didn't fit the expectations of others, and he seemed to be okay with that. Author Rufus Burrows referred to Dr. Johns as "God's Bad Boy"; he was a man of God and a rebel at the same time. "During one of the most dangerous periods of U.S. history…Johns' courage was simply amazing."

Unlike other black religious leaders of his time, Dr. Johns dedicated his entire career to pointing out the injustices faced by black people in this country. He highlighted the role of a church leader as a thought leader and a social activist, laying the foundation for pastors across the nation to use the pulpit as a fighting ground. He made it a "thing" for a preacher to make himself an agent of social change.

Dr. Johns often quoted his mother as saying, "If you see a good fight, get in it." He did that.

Discussion Guide

Chapter 1 Discussion Questions

1. One of Vernon Johns' grandfathers was white; the other was black. Both were punished for killing someone. How do you think this impacted Dr. Johns?
2. How do you think Dr. Johns's family history influenced his ideas about race?
3. Vernon Johns and his sister went to a one-room schoolhouse. What are the advantages of having children of different ages in the same classroom? What are the disadvantages?
4. As a teenager, Vernon had to leave school to take care of his family. Was this the right choice? Based on what you read about his family, can you think of any other alternatives?

Chapter 2 Discussion Questions

1. Willie Johns was a poor man, but he was a positive role model for his son. What does it take to become a positive role model?

2. When chattel slavery ended in America, many schools were created to train freedmen to become teachers and preachers. Why do you think they focused on these two professions?
3. In Chicago in 1919, everything was integrated except the beaches. Why do you think the beaches remained segregated?

Chapter 3 Discussion Questions

1. Johns was in Harlem during the Harlem Renaissance, which was focused on the arts (art, music, dance, literature). How are the arts related to religion?
2. How can people who live in cities (urban) and people who farm (rural) help each other?
3. People were upset with Rev. Johns for running a fish business while he was the pastor of a church. Explain why you think this was or was not an appropriate choice.
4. Dr. Johns believed that all blacks should run some type of small business to overcome poverty. Do you agree or disagree? Explain your position.

Chapter 4 Discussion Questions

1. As a college president, Dr. Johns was raising chickens inside classrooms. Why did people complain about this? What is your opinion on the matter?
2. Student strikes have sometimes been successful in the past. Would they work today? What types of student protests may be more effective?
3. What does it mean to "fail up"? How did Dr. Johns

continue to "fail up" at Virginia Theological Seminary?

Chapter 5 Discussion Questions

1. Do you agree that people would be better off if they knew how to grow their own food and build their own shelter? Why or why not?

Chapter 6 Discussion Questions

1. Would you buy clothes or shoes in a store that wouldn't let you try them on? What if they sold items that you couldn't buy anywhere else? Justify your response.
2. Should churches get involved with social and political issues? Why or why not?
3. Dr. Johns resigned from his job at Dexter Avenue Baptist Church. Why do you think he hesitated to leave after they accepted his resignation?
4. Do you think Dr. Johns lost his jobs mostly because of his ideas and or because of his bad temper? Support your position.

Chapter 7 Discussion Questions

1. Why do you think Rev. Abernathy invited both men to dinner at his house on the same night?
2. Dr. Johns wanted to drive to Montgomery with Martin Luther King, Jr. What do you think he wanted to talk about?
3. It was clear that Dr. King respected Dr. Johns. Why

do you think he failed to invite Dr. Johns to the 1963 March on Washington?

4. Preachers often borrow sermon ideas from one another. Do you see a problem with this? Should they reveal that their words came from someone else?

Chapter 8 Discussion Questions

1. Why do you think Dr. Johns gave sermons in his store? What did he hope to accomplish by preaching to people who didn't normally go to church?

2. Dr. Johns used violence against the burglars that broke into his store. Would Dr. King approve of this behavior? How do you know?

Chapter 9 Discussion Questions

1. A legacy is what a person leaves behind after they pass away. Do you agree that everyone should leave some type of legacy?

2. What is your definition of 'freedom?' Is having money the same as economic freedom? Is there more to it?

3. Why do you think Barbara Johns has been left out of Civil Rights history? Do you believe it's because of her age or something else?

4. The word "fight" is used here in a positive way. Can you think of other examples where fighting is a good thing?

5. Do you agree or disagree that people are responsible for their own freedom? What kind of things should people do to keep themselves free?

6. What do you think is the most important aspect of Vernon Johns's legacy?

References

Abdul-Jabar, Kareem (Executive Producer) & Fink, Kenneth.(1994, January 15). "The Vernon Johns Story". [Television Broadcast].

Abernathy, Ralph David. (1989). And The Walls Came Tumbling Down: An Autobiography. New York: Harper and Row.

Anderson, James D. (1988). The Education of Blacks in the South, 1860-1935. Chapel Hill, NC: University of North Carolina Press.

Anderson, Jervis. (1981). This Was Harlem: A Cultural Portrait 1900-1950. New York: Farrar, Straus & Giroux.

Bailey, A. Peter. (1993, December-January). "The Vernon Johns Story." American Visions, Vol.8 no. 6.

Boddie, Charles Emerson. (1972). God's Bad Boys. Valley Forge, PA: Judson Press.

Branch, Taylor. (1988). Parting the Waters: America in the King Years, 1954-63. New York: A Touchstone Book, Simon and Schuster.

Cooney, P.L. & Powell, H. W. (1998). The life and times of the prophet Vernon Johns. Retrieved from http://www.vernon-johns.org/tcal001/vjtofc.html.

Dabney, Virginius. (1971). Virginia: The New Dominion. Garden City, NY: Doubleday and Co., Inc.

Gandy, Samuel L. (1977). Human Possibilities: A Vernon Johns Reader. Gandy, Samuel Lucius (ed.). Washington, D.C.: Hoffman Press.

Hamilton, Charles V. (1991). Adam Clayton Powell, Jr.: The Political Biography of An American Dilemma. New York: Atheneum.

Kanefield, Teri. (2014). The Girl from the Tar Paper School:Barbara Rose Johns and the Advent of the Civil Rights Movement, New York: Harry N. Abrams.

King, Martin Luther, Jr. (with Clayton Riley). (1958). Stride Toward Freedom: The Montgomery Story. New York: Harper and Row.

Luker, Ralph E. (1996). Historical Dictionary of the Civil Rights Movement, 1941-1995. The Scarecrow Press, Inc..

Luker, Ralph (2003). "Johns the Baptist". Retrieved from http://www.ralphluker.com/vjohns/baptist.html

Reavis, Ralph. (1990). Virginia Seminary: A Journey of Black Independence. Bedford, VA: The Print Shop.

Schneider, Gregory (February 23, 2017). "Virginia dedicates state office building in honor of civil rights pioneer". Washington Post. Retrieved from https://www.washingtonpost.com/local/virginia-politics/virginia-dedicates-state-office-building-in-honor-of-civil-rights-pioneer/2017/02/23/3558aa5c-f9d9-11e6-be05-1a3817ac21a5_story.html.

Smith, Bob. (1965). They Closed Their Schools: Prince Edward County, Virginia, 1951-64. Chapel Hill, NC: University of North Carolina Press.

Stokes, John A. (with Lois Wolfe). (2008). Students on Strike: Jim Crow, Civil Rights, Brown, and Me, A Memoir. Washington, DC: National Geographic Press, 2008

Wally G. Vaughan, ed. (1999). Reflections on our Pastor. Richard W. Wills. Dover: Majority Press.

About the Author

Simone (Ray) Thomas is a native of Denver, CO. She is an alumna of Tuskegee University and received a doctorate in Education from the University of Memphis. She has two children- Amani Simone and Daryl Ramon, Jr.- and one granddaughter, Aniya Simone. She has worked in Education since 1997 and currently lives in Alabama.

Simone's "Tuskegee Lake Poem", was published in the *Agnieska's Dowry* collection in 1997. She has since edited a range of projects and written for local publications in Chicago and Memphis.

The UNHEARD OF imprint was created to illuminate the often overlooked historic contributions of black Americans. Other UNHEARD OF books include *365 Days of Black Men in History* (2016) and *Driven* (2022).

Contact unheardbooks@gmail.com for more information.

Lightning Source UK Ltd.
Milton Keynes UK
UKHW040651050922
408358UK00001B/257

9 798985 782806